ALSO BY MICHAEL JACKSON

moonwalk

dancing the dream

POEMS & REFLECTIONS

WRITTEN BY

michael jackson

doubleday

NEW YORK LONDON TORONTO SYDNEY AUCKLAND

dancing the dream

POEMS AND REFLECTIONS

WRITTEN BY

MICHAEL JACKSON

PUBLISHED BY DOUBLEDAY
A DIVISION OF BANTAM DOUBLEDAY DELL
PUBLISHING GROUP, INC. 666 FIFTH AVENUE,
NEW YORK, NEW YORK 10103

DOUBLEDAY AND THE PORTRAYAL OF AN ANCHOR
WITH A DOLPHIN ARE TRADEMARKS OF
DOUBLEDAY, A DIVISION OF BANTAM DOUBLEDAY
DELL PUBLISHING GROUP, INC.

LIBRARY OF CONGRESS CATALOGING-IN-
PUBLICATION DATA
JACKSON, MICHAEL, 1958–
    DANCING THE DREAM / MICHAEL JACKSON. — 1ST ED.
        P.   CM.
    I. TITLE.
    ML420.J175A3   1992
    818'.5409—DC20   91-48268
                                                    CIP
                                                    MN

ISBN 0-385-42277-6

PRINTED IN
JULY 1992

10 9 8 7 6 5 4 3 2 1
FIRST EDITION

*Dedicated to
Mother
with love.*

DEEPAK,

THANK YOU FOR YOUR INSPIRATION

AND YOUR LOVE.

introduction

When I hear the name Michael Jackson, I think of brilliance, of dazzling stars, lasers and deep emotions. I adore Michael Jackson. I think he is one of the world's biggest and greatest stars, and it just so happens that he is one of the most gifted music makers the world has ever known.

What makes Michael more unique may be the fact that all of his accomplishments, his rewards, have not altered his sensitivity and concern for the welfare of others, or his intense caring and love for his family and friends, and especially all the children the world over.

I think Michael is like litmus paper. He is always trying to learn. He is so intelligent that he is alarmingly bright. He is also very curious and wants to draw from people who have survived. People who have lasted. He is not really of this planet. He is filled with deep emotions that create an unearthly, special, innocent, childlike, wise man that is Michael Jackson. I think Michael appeals to the child in all of us, and I think he has the quality of innocence that we would all like to obtain or to have kept.

He has one of the sharpest wits, he is intelligent and he is cunning—that is a strange word to use about him, because it implies deviousness and he is one of the least devious people I have ever met in my life. He is honesty personified—painfully honest—and vulnerable to the point of pain. He is so giving of himself that, at times, he leaves very little to protect that beautiful inner core that is the essence of him. That is the thing that I love so much about him and that makes the world identify with him in the way it does.

Michael Jackson is, indeed, an international favorite for all ages, an incredible force of incredible energy. In the art of music, he is a pacesetter for quality of production, in the vanguard for high standards of entertainment. What is a genius? What is a living legend? What is a megastar? Michael Jackson—that's all. And just when you think you know him, he gives you more . . .

I think he is one of the finest people to hit this planet, and, in my estimation, he is the true King of Pop, Rock and Soul.

—ELIZABETH TAYLOR

dancing the dream

Consciousness expresses itself through creation. This world we live in is the dance of the creator. Dancers come and go in the twinkling of an eye but the dance lives on. On many an occasion when I'm dancing, I've felt touched by something sacred. In those moments, I've felt my spirit soar and become one with everything that exists. I become the stars and the moon. I become the lover and the beloved. I become the victor and the vanquished. I become the master and the slave. I become the singer and the song. I become the knower and the known. I keep on dancing and then, it is the eternal dance of creation. The creator and creation merge into one wholeness of joy.

I keep on dancing and dancing . . . . and dancing, until there is only . . . . . . the dance.

— MICHAEL JACKSON

PLANET *earth*

Planet Earth, my home, my place
A capricious anomaly in the sea of space
Planet Earth, are you just
Floating by, a cloud of dust
A minor globe about to bust
A piece of metal bound to rust
A speck of matter in a mindless void
A lonely spaceship, a large asteroid

Cold as a rock without a hue
Held together with a bit of glue
Something tells me this isn't true
You are my sweetheart, soft and blue
Do you care, have you a part
In the deepest emotions of my own heart
Tender with breezes, caressing and whole
Alive with music, haunting my soul.

In my veins I've felt the mystery
Of corridors of time, books of history
Life songs of ages throbbing in my blood
Have danced the rhythm of the tide and flood
Your misty clouds, your electric storm

Were turbulent tempests in my own form
I've licked the salt, the bitter, the sweet
Of every encounter, of passion, of heat
Your riotous color, your fragrance, your taste
Have thrilled my senses beyond all haste
In your beauty I've known the how
Of timeless bliss, this moment of now.

Planet Earth, are you just
Floating by, a cloud of dust
A minor globe about to bust
A piece of metal bound to rust
A speck of matter in a mindless void
A lonely spaceship, a large asteroid

Cold as a rock without a hue
Held together with a bit of glue
Something tells me this isn't true
You are my sweetheart, gentle and blue
Do you care, have you a part
In the deepest emotions of my own heart
Tender with breezes, caressing and whole
Alive with music, haunting my soul.

Planet Earth, gentle and blue
With all my heart, I love you.

part 1

MAGICAL *child*

Once there was a child and he was free
Deep inside, he felt the laughter
The mirth and play of nature's glee
He was not troubled by thoughts of hereafter
Beauty, love was all he'd see

He knew his power was the power of God
He was so sure, they considered him odd
This power of innocence, of compassion, of light
Threatened the priests and created a fright
In endless ways they sought to dismantle
This mysterious force which they could not handle

In endless ways they tried to destroy
His simple trust, his boundless joy
His invincible armor was a shield of bliss
Nothing could touch it, no venom, no hiss

The child remained in a state of grace
He wasn't confined in time or place
In Technicolor dreams, he frolicked and played
While acting his part, in Eternity he stayed

Soothsayers came and fortunes were told
Some were vehement, others were bold
In denouncing this child, this perplexing creature
With the rest of the world he shared no feature
Is he real? He is so strange
His unpredictable nature knows no range
He puzzles us so, is he straight?
What's his destiny? What's his fate?

And while they whispered and conspired
Through endless rumors to get him tired
To kill his wonder, trample him near
Burn his courage, fuel his fear
The child remained just simple, sincere

All he wanted was the mountain high
Color the clouds, paint the sky
Beyond these boundaries, he wanted to fly
In nature's scheme, never to die

Don't stop this child, he's the father of man
Don't cross his way, he's part of the plan
I am that Child, but so are you
You've just forgotten, just lost the clue

Inside your heart sits a Seer
Between his thoughts, he can hear
A melody simple but wondrously clear
The music of life, so precious, so dear

If you could for one moment know
This spark of creation, this exquisite glow
You would come and dance with me
Kindle this fire so we could see
All the children of the Earth
Weave their magic and give new birth
To a world of freedom with no pain
A world of joy, much more sane

Deep inside, you know it's true
Just find that child, it's hiding in you.

WINGS *without* ME

It was August, and I was looking up at the sky. With one hand shielding my eyes, I made out a falcon soaring on the currents of hot swirling air. Higher and higher it spiraled, until with one unearthly shriek, it disappeared.

All at once I felt left behind. "Why did you grow wings without me?" I mourned. Then my spirit said, "The falcon's way is not the only way. Your thoughts are as free as any bird." So I shut my eyes and my spirit took off, spiraling as high as the falcon and then beyond, so that I was looking down over the whole earth. But something was wrong. Why did I feel so cold and alone?

"You grew wings without me," my heart said. "What good is freedom without love?" So I went quietly to the bed of a sick child and sang him a lullaby. He fell asleep smiling, and my heart took off, joining my spirit as it circled over the earth. I was free and loving, but still something was wrong.

"You grew wings without me," my body said. "Your flights are only imagination." So I looked into books that I had ignored before and read about saints in every age who actually flew. In India, Persia, China, and Spain (even in Los Angeles!), the power of spirit has reached, not just into the heart, but into every cell of the body. "As if carried aloft by a great eagle," Saint Teresa said, "my ecstasy lifted me into the air."

I began to believe in this amazing feat, and for the first time, I didn't feel left behind. I was the falcon and the child and the saint. In my eyes their lives became sacred, and the truth came home: When all life is seen as divine, everyone grows wings.

DANCE OF *life*

I cannot escape the moon. Its soft beams push aside the curtains at night. I don't even have to see it—a cool blue energy falls across my bed and I am up. I race down the dark hall and swing open the door, not to leave home but to go back to it. "Moon, I'm here!" I shout.

"Good," she replies. "Now give us a little dance."

But my body has started moving long before she says anything. When did it start? I can't remember—my body has always been moving. Since childhood I have reacted to the moon this way, as her favorite lunatic, and not just hers. The stars draw me near, close enough so that I see through their twinkling act. They're dancing, too, doing a soft molecular jiggle that makes my carbon atoms jump in time.

With my arms flung wide, I head for the sea, which brings out another dance in me. Moon dancing is slow inside, and soft as blue shadows on the lawn. When the surf booms, I hear the heart of the earth, and the tempo picks up. I feel the dolphins leaping in the white foam, trying to fly, and almost flying when the waves curl high to the heavens. Their tails leave arcs of light as plankton glow in the waves. A school of minnows rises up, flashing silver in the moonlight like a new constellation.

"Ah!" the sea says. "Now we're gathering a crowd."

I run along the beach, catching waves with one foot and dodging them with the other. I hear faint popping sounds—a hundred panicky sand crabs are ducking into their holes, just in case. But I'm racing now, sometimes on my toes, sometimes running flat-out.

I throw my head back and a swirling nebula says, "Fast now, twirl!"

Grinning, ducking my head for balance, I start to spin as wildly

as I can. This is my favorite dance, because it contains a secret. The faster I twirl, the more I am still inside. My dance is all motion without, all silence within. As much as I love to make music, it's the unheard music that never dies. And silence is my real dance, though it never moves. It stands aside, my choreographer of grace, and blesses each finger and toe.

I have forgotten the moon now and the sea and the dolphins, but I am in their joy more than ever. As far away as a star, as near as a grain of sand, the presence rises, shimmering with light. I could be in it forever, it is so loving and warm. But touch it once, and light shoots forth from the stillness. It quivers and thrills me, and I know my fate is to show others that this silence, this light, this blessing is my dance. I take this gift only to give it again.

"Quick, give!" says the light.

As never before, I try to obey, inventing new steps, new gestures of joy. All at once I sense where I am, running back up the hill. The light in my bedroom is on. Seeing it brings me back down. I begin to feel my pounding heart, the drowsiness in my arms, the warm blood in my legs. My cells want to dance slower. "Can we walk a little?" they ask. "It's been kind of wild."

"Sure." I laugh, slowing to an easy amble.

I turn the doorknob, panting lightly, glad to be tired. Crawling back into bed, I remember something that I always wonder at. They say that some of the stars that we see overhead aren't really there. Their light takes millions of years to reach us, and all we are doing is looking into the past, into a bygone moment when those stars could still shine.

"So what does a star do after it quits shining?" I ask myself. "Maybe it dies."

"Oh no," a voice in my head says. "A star can never die. It just turns into a smile and melts back into the cosmic music, the dance of life." I like that thought, the last one I have before my eyes close. With a smile, I melt back into the music myself.

WHEN *babies* SMILE

When dreamers dream and kiss their lover
And rainbows weave and splash their color
Those are moments so gloriously alive
We take the plunge, take the dive
Into the abyss
We are suspended awhile
Those are moments when babies smile.

Those are moments when fate is unsealed
Nothing is impossible and we are healed
We can soar, we can fly
Walk on fire, navigate the sky
In the light of a glittering star
There's no distance, nothing is far
Those are moments of innocent guile
In the glow
We are suspended awhile
Those are moments when babies smile.

Those are moments when the heart is tender
When seascapes gleam in magnificent splendor
When the laughter of Heaven reverberates the Earth
And we are renewed in a new birth
In a timeless Eternity

In the angels' fraternity
We romp and roll
The playground of our soul
In the twilight
We are suspended awhile
Those are moments when babies smile.

Those are moments we're one with God
All is well, nothing is odd
In silent reflection
We feel our perfection
We are the source, we are the crucible
Nothing can hurt us, for we are invincible
There is no sin, there is no sinner
We can only win, we have felt the glimmer
In the bliss
We're floating awhile
Those are moments when babies smile.

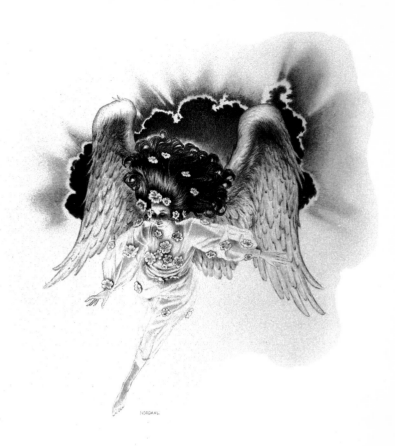

Kingdoms topple, lose their class
Civilizations crumble, ages pass
Turbulent tempests ravage the seas
Violent killings, despite our pleas
But dewdrops sparkle when children play
Tyrants cry, there's nothing to slay
Fairies dance and goblins sing
All are crowned, all are king
In the Garden
We frolic awhile
Those are moments when babies smile.

BUT THE *heart* SAID NO

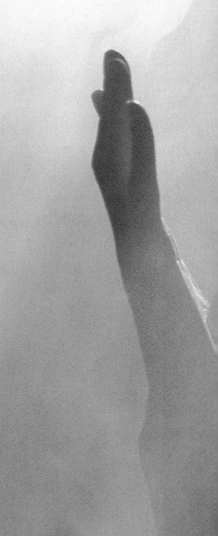

They saw the poor living in cardboard shacks, so they knocked the shacks down and built projects. Huge blocks of cement and glass towered over asphalt parking lots. Somehow it wasn't much like home, even home in a shack. "What do you expect?" they asked impatiently. "You're too poor to live like us. Until you can do better for yourselves, you should be grateful, shouldn't you?"

The head said yes, but the heart said no.

They needed more electricity in the city, so they found a mountain stream to dam. As the waters rose, dead rabbits and deer floated by; baby birds too young to fly drowned in the nest while mother birds cried helplessly. "It's not a pretty sight," they said, "but now a million people can run their air conditioners all summer. That's more important than one mountain stream, isn't it?"

The head said yes, but the heart said no.

They saw oppression and terrorism in a far-off land, so they made war against it. Bombs reduced the country to rubble. Its population cowered in fear, and every day more villagers were buried in rough wooden coffins. "You have to be prepared to make sacrifices," they said. "If some innocent bystanders get hurt, isn't that just the price one must pay for peace?"

The head said yes, but the heart said no.

The years rolled by and they got old. Sitting in their comfortable houses, they took stock. "We've had a good life," they said, "and we did the right thing." Their children looked down and asked why poverty, pollution, and war were still unsolved. "You'll find out soon enough," they replied. "Human beings are weak and selfish. Despite our best efforts, these problems will never really end."

The head said yes, but the children looked into their hearts and whispered, "No!"

children OF THE WORLD

Children of the world, we'll do it
We'll meet on endless shores
Making sandcastles and floating our boats
While people fight and defend their point of view
Forever putting on masks that are new
We'll swing the tide of time and do it.

Children of the world, we'll do it
With song and dance and innocent bliss
And the soft caress of a loving kiss
We'll do it.

While traders trade and haggle their price
And politicians try so hard to be nice
We'll meet on endless shores and floating our boats
We'll do it.

While lawyers argue and doctors treat
Stockbrokers quote the price on meat
While preachers preach and ring the bell
Carpetbaggers with something to sell
We'll sing and dance in innocent bliss
With the soft caress of a loving kiss
We'll do it
Meeting on endless shores
Making sandcastles and floating our boats
We'll do it.

We'll ride a rainbow, a cloud, a storm
Flying in the wind, we'll change our form
We'll touch the stars, embrace the moon
We'll break the barrier and be there soon

While architects plan their buildings high
And trade unions raise their hue and cry
While boardroom squabbles generate heat
And in secret places dealers meet
We'll sing and dance in innocent bliss
With the soft caress of a loving kiss
We'll do it.

While philosophers grapple and continue to tackle
Endless dilemmas of body and mind
Physicists wander, continue to ponder
Perennial questions of space and time
Archaeologists survey, continue to dig
Bygone treasures small and big
Psychologists probe, analyze the tears
Of hysterical notions, phobias, fears

While priests take confession
In a serious session
And people struggle
In the hustle and bustle
In the noise and din
On the meaning of sin
We'll touch the stars, embrace the moon
Break the barrier, arrive there soon
Ride the rainbow, the cloud, the storm
Flying in the wind, changing our form

Children of the world, we'll do it
With song and dance and innocent bliss
The soft caress of a loving kiss
We'll do it.

SO THE *elephants* MARCH

A curious fact about elephants is this: In order to survive, they mustn't fall down. Every other animal can stumble and get back up again. But an elephant always stands up, even to sleep. If one of the herd slips and falls, it is helpless. It lies on its side, a prisoner of its own weight. Although the other elephants will press close around it in distress and try to lift it up again, there isn't usually much they can do. With slow heaving breaths, the fallen elephant dies. The others stand vigil, then slowly move on.

This is what I learned from nature books, but I wonder if they are right. Isn't there another reason why elephants can't fall down? Perhaps they have decided not to. Not to fall down is their mission. As the wisest and most patient of animals, they made a pact—I imagine it was eons ago, when the ice ages were ending. Moving in great herds across the face of the earth, the elephants first spied tiny men prowling the tall grasses with their flint spears.

"What fear and anger this creature has," the elephants thought. "But he is going to inherit the earth. We are wise enough to see that. Let us set an example for him."

Then the elephants put their grizzled heads together and pondered. What kind of example could they show to man? They could show him that their power was much greater than his, for that was certainly true. They could display their anger before him, which was terrible enough to uproot whole forests. Or they could lord it over man through fear, trampling his fields and crushing his huts.

In moments of great frustration, wild elephants will do all of these things, but as a group, putting their heads together, they decided that man would learn best from a kinder message.

"Let us show him our reverence for life," they said. And from that day on, elephants have been silent, patient, peaceful creatures. They let men ride them and harness them like slaves. They permit children to laugh at their tricks in the circus, exiled from the great African plains where they once lived as lords.

But the elephants' most important message is in their movement. For they know that to live is to move. Dawn after dawn, age after age, the herds march on, one great mass of life that never falls down, an unstoppable force of peace.

Innocent animals, they do not suspect that after all this time, they will fall from a bullet by the thousands. They will lie in the dust, mutilated by our shameless greed. The great males fall first, so that their tusks can be made into trinkets. Then the females fall, so that men may have trophies. The babies run screaming from the smell of their own mothers' blood, but it does them no good to run from the guns. Silently, with no one to nurse them, they will die, too, and all their bones bleach in the sun.

In the midst of so much death, the elephants could just give up. All they have to do is drop to the ground. That is enough. They don't need a bullet: Nature has given them the dignity to lie down and find their rest. But they remember their ancient pact and their pledge to us, which is sacred.

So the elephants march on, and every tread beats out words in the dust: "Watch, learn, love. Watch, learn, love." Can you hear them? One day in shame, the ghosts of ten thousand lords of the plains will say, "We do not hate you. Don't you see at last? We were willing to fall, so that you, dear small ones, will never fall again."

THE *boy* AND THE PILLOW

A wise father wanted to teach his young son a lesson. "Here is a pillow covered in silk brocade and stuffed with the rarest goose down in the land," he said. "Go to town and see what it will fetch."

First the boy went to the marketplace, where he saw a wealthy feather merchant. "What will you give me for this pillow?" he asked.

The merchant narrowed his eyes. "I will give you fifty gold ducats, for I see that this is a rare treasure indeed."

The boy thanked him and went on. Next he saw a farmer's wife peddling vegetables by the side of the road. "What will you give me for this pillow?" he asked. She felt it and exclaimed, "How soft it is! I'll give you one piece of silver, for I long to lay my weary head on such a pillow."

The boy thanked her and walked on. Finally he saw a young peasant girl washing the steps of a church. "What will you give me for this pillow?" he asked. Looking at him with a strange smile, she replied, "I'll give you a penny, for I can see that your pillow is hard compared to these stones." Without hesitation, the boy laid the pillow at her feet.

When he got home, he said to his father, "I have gotten the best price for your pillow." And he held out the penny.

"What?" his father exclaimed. "That pillow was worth a hundred gold ducats at least."

"That's what a wealthy merchant saw," the boy said, "but being greedy, he offered me fifty. I got a better offer than that. A farmer's wife offered me one piece of silver."

"Are you mad?" his father said. "When is one piece of silver worth more than fifty gold ducats?"

"When it's offered out of love," the boy replied. "If she had given me more, she wouldn't have been able to feed her children. Yet I got a better offer than that. I saw a peasant girl washing the steps of a church who offered me this penny."

"You have lost your wits completely," his father said, shaking his head. "When is a penny worth more than a piece of silver?"

"When its offered out of devotion," the boy replied. "For she was laboring for her Lord, and the steps of His house seemed softer than any pillow. Poorer than the poorest, she still had time for God. And that is why I offered her the pillow."

At this the wise father smiled and embraced his son, and with a tear in his eye he murmured, "You have learned well."

enough FOR TODAY

Dance rehearsals can go on past midnight, but this time I stopped at ten. "I hope you don't mind," I said, looking up into space, "but that's enough for today."

A voice from the control room spoke. "You okay?"

"A little tired, I guess," I said.

I slipped on a windbreaker and headed down the hall. Running footsteps came up behind me. I was pretty sure who they belonged to. "I know you too well," she said, catching up with me. "What's really wrong?"

I hesitated. "Well, I don't know how this sounds, but I saw a picture today in the papers. A dolphin had drowned in a fishing net. From the way its body was tangled in the lines, you could read so much agony. Its eyes were vacant, yet there was still that smile, the one dolphins never lose, even when they die . . ." My voice trailed off.

She put her hand lightly in mine. "I know, I know."

"No, you don't know all of it yet. It's not just that I felt sad, or had to face the fact that an innocent being had died. Dolphins love to dance—of all the creatures in the sea, that's their mark. Asking nothing from us, they cavort in the waves while we marvel. They race ahead of ships, not to get there first but to tell us, 'It's all meant to be play. Keep to your course, but dance while you do it.'

"So there I was, in the middle of rehearsal, and I thought, 'They're killing a dance.' And then it seemed only right to stop. I can't keep the dance from being killed, but at least I can pause in memory, as one dancer to another. Does that make any sense?"

Her eyes were tender. "Sure, in its way. Probably we'll wait years before everyone agrees on how to solve this thing. So many interests are involved. But it's too frustrating waiting for improvements tomorrow. Your heart wanted to have its say now."

"Yes," I said, pushing the door open for her. "I just had this feeling, and that's enough for today."

MARK OF THE *ancients*

He had lived in the desert all his life, but for me it was all new. "See that footprint in the sand?" he asked, pointing to a spot by the cliff. I looked as close as I could. "No, I don't see anything."

"That's just the point." He laughed. "Where you can't see a print, that's where the Ancient Ones walked."

We went on a little farther, and he pointed to an opening, high up on the sandstone wall. "See that house up there?" he asked. I squinted hard. "There's nothing to see."

"You're a good student." He smiled. "Where there's no roof or chimney, that's where the Ancient Ones are most likely to have lived."

We rounded a bend, and before us was spread a fabulous sight — thousands upon thousands of desert flowers in bloom. "Can you see any missing?" he asked me. I shook my head. "It's just wave after wave of loveliness."

"Yes," he said in a low voice. "Where nothing is missing, that's where the Ancient Ones harvested the most."

I thought about all this, about how generations once lived in harmony with the earth, leaving no marks to scar the places they inhabited. At camp that night I said, "You left out one thing."

"What's that?" he asked.

"Where are the Ancient Ones buried?"

Without reply, he poked his stick into the fire. A bright flame shot up, licked the air, and disappeared. My teacher gave me a glance to ask if I understood this lesson. I sat very still, and my silence told him I did.

HEAL THE *world*

There's a place in your heart
And I know that it is love
And this place could be much brighter
Than tomorrow
And if you really try
You'll find there's no need to cry
In this place I feel there's no hurt or sorrow

There are ways to get there
If you care enough for the living
Make a little space
Make a better place
Heal the world
Make it a better place
For you and for me
And the entire human race

There are people dying
If you care enough for the living
Make a better place
For you and for me

If you want to know why, there's a love that cannot lie
Love is strong, it cares for only joyful giving
If we try, we shall see
In this bliss we cannot feel
Fear or dread

Then we just stop existing and start living
Then it feels that always
Love's enough for us growing
Make a better world
Make a better world
Heal the world
Make it a better place
For you and for me
And the entire human race

There are people dying
If you care enough for the living
Make a better place for you and for me

And the dream we were conceived in
Will reveal its joyful face
And the world we once believed in
Will shine again in grace

Then why do we keep strangling life
Wound this Earth, crucify its soul
Tho it's plain to see
This world is heavenly
We could be God's glow
We could fly so high
Let our spirit never die

In my heart I feel you are all my brothers
Create a world with no fear
Together we'll cry happy tears
So that nations turn their swords into plowshares
We could really get there
If you cared enough for the living
Make a little space
To make a better place
Heal the world
Make it a better place

For you and for me
And the entire human race

There are people dying
If you care enough for the living
Make a better place
For you and for me
Heal the world
Make it a better place
For you and for me
And the entire human race

There are people dying
If you care enough for the living
Make a better place
For you and for me

Heal the world
Make it a better place
For you and for me
And the entire human race

There are people dying
If you care enough for the living
Make a better place
For you and for me

There are people dying
If you care enough for the living
Make a better place
For you and for me

There are people dying
If you care enough for the living
Make a better place
For you and for me
For you and for me
For you and for me
For you and for me
For you and for me
You and for me
You and for me

children

Children show me in their playful smiles the divine in everyone. This simple goodness shines straight from their hearts. This has so much to teach. If a child wants chocolate ice cream, he just asks for it. Adults get tangled up in complications over whether to eat the ice cream or not. A child simply enjoys.

What we need to learn from children isn't childish. Being with them connects us to the deep wisdom of life, which is everpresent and only asks to be lived. Now, when the world is so confused and its problems so complicated, I feel we need our children more than ever. Their natural wisdom points the way to solutions that lie, waiting to be recognized, within our own hearts.

mother

Eons of time I've been gestating
To take a form been hesitating
From the unmanifest this cosmic conception
On this earth a fantastic reception
And then one fateful August morn
From your being I was born
With tender love you nurtured a seed
To your own distress you paid no heed
Unmindful of any risk and danger
You decided upon this lonely stranger

Rainbows, clouds, the deep blue sky
Glittering birds that fly on high
Out of fragments you've made my whole
From the elements you fashioned my soul
Mother dear, you gave me life
Because of you, no struggle or strife
You gave me joy and position
Cared for me without condition
And if I ever change this world
It's from the emotions you've unfurl'd
Your compassion is so sweet and dear
Your finest feelings I can hear
I can sense your faintest notion
The wondrous magic of your love potion

And now that I have come so far
Met with every king and czar
Encountered every color and creed
Of every passion, every greed
I go back to that starry night
With not a fear for muscle or might
You taught me how to stand and fight
For every single wrong and right
Every day without a hold
I will treasure what you've mold
I will remember every kiss
Your sweet words I'll never miss
No matter where I go from here
You're in my heart, my mother dear.

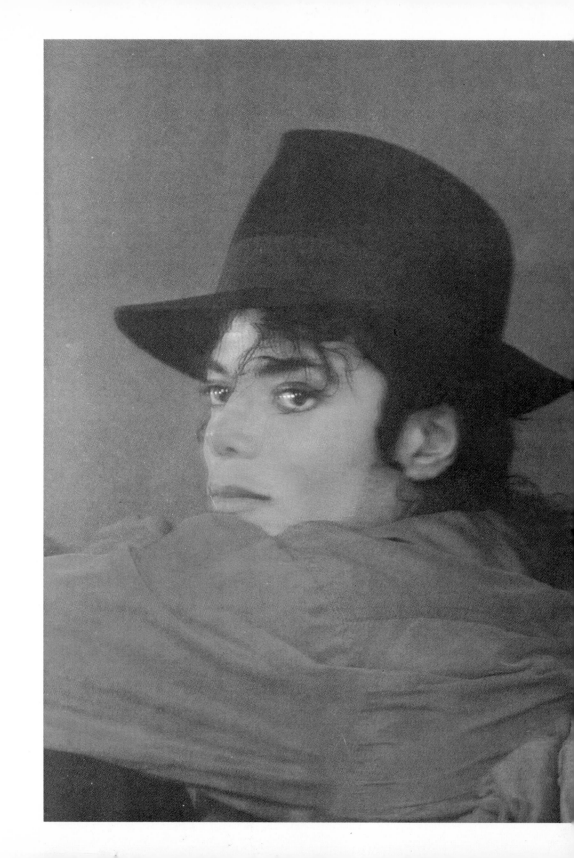

magic

My idea of magic doesn't have much to do with stage tricks and illusions. The whole world abounds in magic. When a whale plunges out of the sea like a newborn mountain, you gasp in unexpected delight. What magic! But a toddler who sees his first tadpole flashing in a mud puddle feels the same thrill. Wonder fills his heart, because he has glimpsed for an instant the playfulness of life.

When I see the clouds whisked away from a snow-capped peak, I feel like shouting, "Bravo!" Nature, the best of all magicians, has delivered another thrill. She has exposed the real illusion, our inability to be amazed by her wonders. Every time the sun rises, Nature is repeating one command: "Behold!" Her magic is infinitely lavish, and in return all we have to do is appreciate it.

What delight Nature must feel when she makes stars out of swirling gas and empty space. She flings them like spangles from a velvet cape, a billion reasons for us to awaken in pure joy. When we open our hearts and appreciate all she has given us, Nature finds her reward. The sound of applause rolls across the universe, and she bows.

THE *fish* THAT WAS THIRSTY

One night a baby fish was sleeping under some coral when God appeared to him in a dream. "I want you to go forth with a message to all the fish in the sea," God said.

"What should I tell them?" the little fish asked.

"Just tell them you're thirsty," God replied. "And see what they do." Then without another word, He disappeared.

The next morning the little fish woke up and remembered his dream. "What a strange thing God wants me to do," he thought to himself. But as soon as he saw a large tuna swimming by, the little fish piped up, "Excuse me, but I'm thirsty."

"Then you must be a fool," the tuna said. And with a disdainful flick of his tail, he swam away.

The little fish did feel rather foolish, but he had his orders. The next fish he saw was a grinning shark. Keeping a safe distance, the little fish called out, "Excuse me, sir, but I'm thirsty."

"Then you must be crazy," the shark replied. Noticing a rather hungry look in the shark's eye, the little fish swam away quickly.

All day he met cod and mackerels and swordfish and groupers, but every time he made his short speech, they turned their backs and would have nothing to do with him. Feeling hopelessly confused, the little fish sought out the wisest creature in the sea, who happened to be an old blue whale with three harpoon scars on his side.

"Excuse me, but I'm thirsty!" the little fish shouted, wondering if the old whale could even see him, he was such a tiny speck. But the wise one stopped in his tracks. "You've seen God, haven't you?" he said.

"How did you know?"

"Because I was thirsty once, too." The old whale laughed.

The little fish looked very surprised. "Please tell me what this message from God means," he implored.

"It means that we are looking for Him in the wrong places," the old whale explained. "We look high and low for God, but somehow He's not there. So we blame Him and tell ourselves that He must have forgotten us. Or else we decide that He left a long time ago, if He was ever around."

"How strange," the little fish said, "to miss what is everywhere."

"Very strange," the old whale agreed. "Doesn't it remind you of fish who say they're thirsty?"

innocence

It's easy to mistake being innocent for being simpleminded or naive. We all want to seem sophisticated; we all want to seem street-smart. To be innocent is to be "out of it."

Yet there is a deep truth in innocence. A baby looks in his mother's eyes, and all he sees is love. As innocence fades away, more complicated things take its place. We think we need to outwit others and scheme to get what we want. We begin to spend a lot of energy protecting ourselves. Then life turns into a struggle. People have no choice but to be street-smart. How else can they survive?

When you get right down to it, survival means seeing things the way they really are and responding. It means being open. And that's what innocence is. It's simple and trusting like a child, not judgmental and committed to one narrow point of view. If you are locked into a pattern of thinking and responding, your creativity gets blocked. You miss the freshness and magic of the moment. Learn to be innocent again, and that freshness never fades.

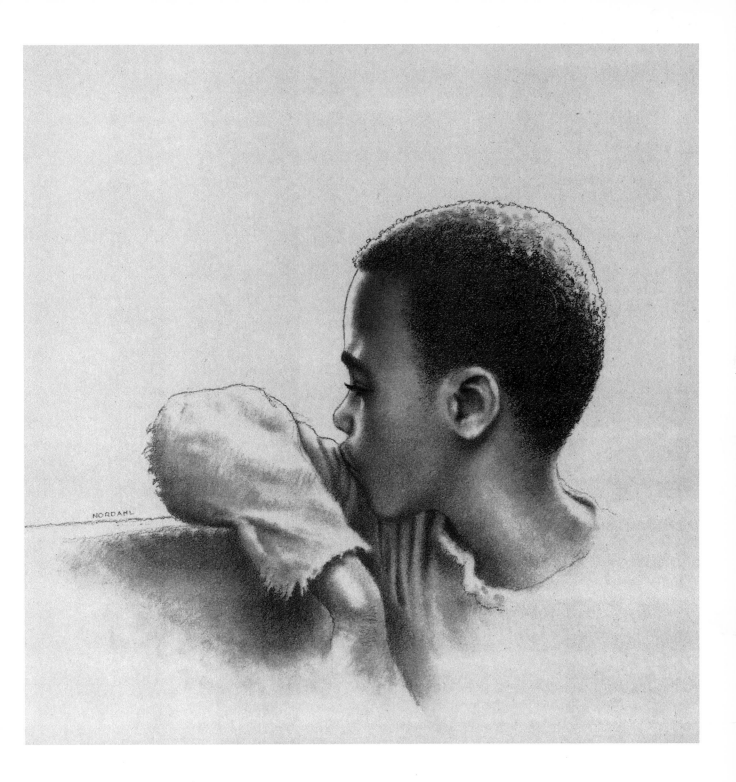

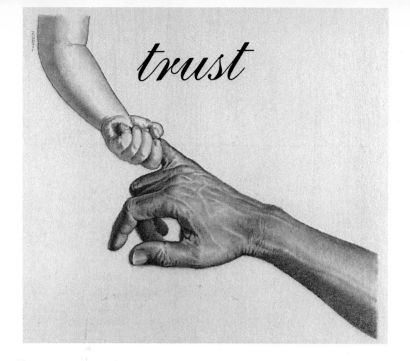

trust

As I was feeding squirrels in the park, I noticed a small one that didn't seem to trust me. While the others came close enough to eat out of my hand, he kept his distance. I threw a peanut his way. He edged up, grabbed it nervously, and ran off. Next time he must have felt less afraid, because he came a little closer. The safer he felt, the more he trusted me. Finally he sat right at my feet, as bold as any squirrel clamoring for the next peanut.

Trust is like that—it always seems to come down to trusting in yourself. Others can't overcome fear for you; you have to do it on your own. It's hard, because fear and doubt hold on tight. We are afraid of being rejected, of being hurt once more. So we keep a safe distance. We think separating ourselves from others will protect us, but that doesn't work, either. It leaves us feeling alone and unloved.

Trusting yourself begins by recognizing that it's okay to be afraid. Having fear is not the problem, because everyone feels anxious and insecure some-times. The problem is not being honest enough to admit your fear. Whenever I accept my own doubt and insecurity, I'm more open to other people. The deeper I go into myself, the stronger I become, because I realize that my real self is much bigger than any fear.

In accepting yourself completely, trust becomes complete. There is no longer any separation between people, because there is no longer any separa-tion inside. In the space where fear used to live, love is allowed to grow.

courage

It's curious what takes courage and what doesn't. When I step out on stage in front of thousands of people, I don't feel that I'm being brave. It can take much more courage to express true feelings to one person. When I think of courage, I think of the Cowardly Lion in *The Wizard of Oz.* He was always running away from danger. He often cried and shook with fear. But he was also sharing his real feelings with those he loved, even though he didn't always like those feelings.

That takes real courage, the courage to be intimate. Expressing your feelings is not the same as falling apart in front of someone else—it's being accepting and true to your heart, whatever it may say. When you have the courage to be intimate, you know who you are, and you're willing to let others see that. It's scary, because you feel so vulnerable, so open to rejection. But without self-acceptance, the other kind of courage, the kind heroes show in movies, seems hollow. In spite of the risks, the courage to be honest and intimate opens the way to self-discovery. It offers what we all want, the promise of love.

love

Love is a funny thing to describe. It's so easy to feel and yet so slippery to talk about. It's like a bar of soap in the bathtub—you have it in your hand until you hold on too tight.

Some people spend their lives looking for love outside themselves. They think they have to grasp it in order to have it. But love slips away like that wet bar of soap.

Holding on to love is not wrong, but you need to learn to hold it lightly, caressingly. Let it fly when it wants. When it's allowed to be free, love is what makes life alive, joyful, and new. It's the juice and energy that motivates my music, my dancing, everything. As long as love is in my heart, it's everywhere.

god

It's strange that God doesn't mind expressing Himself/Herself in all the religions of the world, while people still cling to the notion that their way is the only right way. Whatever you try to say about God, someone will take offense, even if you say everyone's love of God is right for them.

For me the form God takes is not the most important thing. What's most important is the essence. My songs and dances are outlines for Him to come in and fill. I hold out the form, She puts in the sweetness.

I've looked up at the night sky and beheld the stars so intimately close, it was as if my grandmother had made them for me. "How rich, how sumptuous," I thought. In that moment I saw God in His creation. I could as easily have seen Her in the beauty of a rainbow, the grace of a deer bounding through a meadow, the truth of a father's kiss. But for me the sweetest contact with God has no form. I close my eyes, look within, and enter a deep soft silence. The infinity of God's creation embraces me. We are one.

HOW I MAKE *music*

People ask me how I make music. I tell them I just step into it. It's like stepping into a river and joining the flow. Every moment in the river has its song. So I stay in the moment and listen.

What I hear is never the same. A walk through the woods brings a light, crackling song: Leaves rustle in the wind, birds chatter and squirrels scold, twigs crunch underfoot, and the beat of my heart holds it all together. When you join the flow, the music is inside and outside, and both are the same. As long as I can listen to the moment, I'll always have music.

ryan WHITE

Ryan White, symbol of justice
Or child of innocence, messenger of love
Where are you now, where have you gone?

Ryan White, I miss your sunny days
We carelessly frolicked in extended plays

I miss you, Ryan White
I miss your smile, innocent and bright
I miss your glory, I miss your light

Ryan White, symbol of contradiction
Child of Irony, or child of fiction?

I think of your shattered life
Of your struggle, of your strife

While ladies dance in the moonlit night
Champagne parties on chartered cruises
I see your wasted form, your ghostly sight
I feel your festering wounds, your battered bruises

Ryan White, symbol of agony and pain
Of ignorant fear gone insane
In a hysterical society
With free-floating anxiety
And feigned piety

I miss you, Ryan White
You showed us how to stand and fight
In the rain you were a cloudburst of joy
The sparkle of hope in every girl and boy

In the depths of your anguished sorrow
Was the dream of another tomorrow.

THE *elusive* SHADOW

Even tho I traveled far
The door to my soul stayed ajar
In the agony of mortal fear
Your music I did not hear
Thru twisting roads in memory lane
I bore my cross in pain

It was a journey of madness
Of anguish born in sadness
I wandered high and low
Recoiled from every blow
Looking for that stolen nectar
In my heart that long-lost scepter
In all those haunted faces
I searched for my oasis

In a way it was in a drunken craze
A cruel hysteria, a blurry haze
Many a time I tried to break
This shadow following me I could not shake
Many a time in the noisy crowd
In the hustle and bustle of the din so loud
I peered behind to see its trace
I could not lose it in any place

It was only when I broke all ties
After the stillness of the shrieking cries
In the depths of those heaving sighs
The imagined sorrow of a thousand lies
I suddenly stared in your fiery eyes
All at once I found my goal
The elusive shadow was my soul.

ON *children* OF THE WORLD

We have to heal our wounded world. The chaos, despair, and senseless destruction we see

today are a result of the alienation that people feel from each other and their environment.

Often this alienation has its roots in an emotionally deprived childhood. Children have had

their childhood stolen from them. A child's mind needs the nourishment of mystery, magic,

wonder, and excitement. I want my work to help people rediscover the child that's hiding

in them.

two BIRDS

It's hard to tell them what I feel for you. They haven't ever met you, and no one has your picture. So how can they ever understand your mystery? Let's give them a clue:

Two birds sit in a tree. One eats cherries, while the other looks on. Two birds fly through the air. One's song drops like crystal from the sky while the other keeps silent. Two birds wheel in the sun. One catches the light on its silver feathers, while the other spreads wings of invisibility.

It's easy to guess which bird I am, but they'll never find you. Unless . . .

Unless they already know a love that never interferes, that watches from beyond, that breathes free in the invisible air. Sweet bird, my soul, your silence is so precious. How long will it be before the world hears your song in mine?

Oh, that is a day I hunger for!

THE *last* TEAR

Your words stabbed my heart, and I cried tears of pain. "Get out!" I shouted. "These are the last tears I'll ever cry for you." So you left.

I waited hours, but you didn't return. That night by myself I cried tears of frustration.

I waited weeks, but you had nothing to say. Thinking of your voice, I cried tears of loneliness.

I waited months, but you left no sign for me. In the depths of my heart, I cried tears of despair.

How strange that all these tears could not wash away the hurt! Then one thought of love pierced my bitterness. I remembered you in the sunlight, with a smile as sweet as May wine. A tear of gratitude started to fall, and miraculously, you were back. Soft fingers touched my cheek, and you bent over for a kiss.

"Why have you come?" I whispered.

"To wipe away your last tear," you replied. "It was the one you saved for me."

ecstasy

I was born to never die
To live in bliss, to never cry
To speak the truth and never lie
To share my love without a sigh
To stretch my arms without a tie
This is my dance, this is my high
It's not a secret, can't you see
Why can't we all live in ecstasy

Ecstasy   Ecstasy
Why can't we all
Live in Ecstasy.

Without a guilt, without regret
I am here to forget
Tainted memories of imagined sin
In every friend, kith and kin

We have come to celebrate here
The getting rid of every fear
Of every notion, every seed
Of any separation, caste, or creed.

90

This alienation, fragmentation, abomination
Of separation, exploitation, isolation
This cruelty, hysteria, absolute madness
This anger, anxiety, overflowing sadness
Disrupted ecology, wanton destruction
Diseased biology, nature's obstruction
Endangered species, environmental pollution
Holes in the ozone, defying solution
Is not knowing the spark that lights my interior
Is the same fire, glowing in every man, child, and mother superior

We have come to celebrate here
The getting rid of every fear
Of every notion, every seed
Of any separation, caste, or creed.

Feeling free, let us fly
Into the boundless, beyond the sky
For we were born to never die
To live in bliss, to never cry
To speak the truth and never lie
To share our love without a sign
To stretch our arms without a tie

This is our dance, this is our high
It's not a secret, can't you see
Why can't we all live in ecstasy

Ecstasy   Ecstasy
Why can't we all
Live in Ecstasy.

berlin 1989

They hated the Wall, but what could they do? It was too strong to break through.

They feared the Wall, but didn't that make sense? Many who tried to climb over it were killed.

They distrusted the Wall, but who wouldn't? Their enemies refused to tear down one brick, no matter how long the peace talks dragged on.

The Wall laughed grimly. "I'm teaching you a good lesson," it boasted. "If you want to build for eternity, don't bother with stones. Hatred, fear, and distrust are so much stronger."

They knew the Wall was right, and they almost gave up. Only one thing stopped them. They remembered who was on the other side. Grandmother, cousin, sister, wife. Beloved faces that yearned to be seen.

"What's happening?" the Wall asked, trembling. Without knowing what they did, they were looking through the Wall, trying to find their dear ones. Silently, from one person to another, love kept up its invisible work.

"Stop it!" the Wall shrieked. "I'm falling apart." But it was too late. A million hearts had found each other. The Wall had fallen before it came down.

MOTHER *earth*

I was walking along the beach one winter day. Looking down, I saw a wave push a feather up on the sand. It was a sea gull feather stained with oil. I picked it up and felt the dark slick film on my fingers. I couldn't help wondering if the bird had survived. Was it all right out there? I knew it wasn't.

I felt sad to think how carelessly we treat our home. The earth we all share is not just a rock tossed through space but a living, nurturing being. She cares for us; she deserves our care in return. We've been treating Mother Earth the way some people treat a rental apartment. Just trash it and move on.

But there's no place to move on to now. We have brought our garbage and our wars and our racism to every part of the world. We must begin to clean her up, and that means cleaning up our own hearts and minds first, because they led us to poison our dear planet. The sooner we change, the easier it will be to feel our love for Mother Earth and the love she so freely gives back to us.

WISE *little* GIRL

I know a wise little girl who cannot walk. She is confined to a wheel-chair, and she may spend the rest of her life there, since her doctors hold out almost no hope of ever making her paralyzed legs better.

When I first met this little girl, she flashed me a smile that burned me with its blazing happiness. How open she was! She wasn't hiding out from self-pity or asking for approval or protecting herself from a sense of shame. She felt completely innocent about not being able to walk, like a puppy that has no idea if it is a mongrel or champion of the breed.

She made no judgments about herself. That was her wisdom.

I have seen the same wise look in other children, "poor" children as society sees them, because they lack food, money, secure homes, or healthy bodies. By the time they reach a certain age, many of these children grasp just how bad their situation is. The way that adults look at their lives robs them of that first innocence that is so precious and rare. They begin to believe that they should feel bad about themselves; that this is "right."

But this wise little girl, being only four, floated above pity and shame like a carefree sparrow. She took my heart in her hands and made it as weightless as a cotton puff, so that it was impossible for me to even begin to think, "What a terrible thing." All I saw was light and love. In their innocence, very young children know themselves to be light and love. If we will allow them, they can teach us to see ourselves the same way.

One sparkle from a little girl's gaze contains the same knowledge that Nature implants at the heart of every life-form. It is life's silent secret, not to be put into words. It just knows. It knows peace and how not to hurt. It knows that even the least breath is a gesture of gratitude to the Creator. It smiles to be alive, waiting patiently for ages of ignorance and sorrow to pass away like a mirage.

I see this knowledge showing itself in the eyes of children more and more, which makes me think that their innocence is growing stronger. They are going to disarm us adults, and that will be enough to disarm the world. They feel no reason to spoil the environment, and so the environment will be cleaned up without a quarrel. A wise little girl told me the future when she looked at me, so full of peace and contentment. I rejoice in trusting her above all the experts. As light and love drive away our guilt and shame, her prophecy must come true.

I YOU *We*

I said you had to do it. You said you didn't want to. We talked about it, and we agreed that maybe I could help.

I said you were wrong. You insisted you were right. We held each other's hand, and right and wrong disappeared.

I began crying. You began crying, too. We embraced, and between us grew a flower of peace.

How I love this mystery called We! Where does it come from, out of thin air? I thought about this mystery, and I realized something: We must be love's favorite child, because until I reach out for you, We is not even there. It arrives on the wings of tenderness; it speaks through our silent understanding. When I laugh at myself, it smiles. When I forgive you, it dances in jubilation.

So We is not a choice anymore, not if you and I want to grow with one another. We unites us, increases our strength; it picks up our burden when you and I are ready to let it fall. The truth is that you and I would have given up long ago, but We won't let us. It is too wise. "Look into your hearts," it says. "What do you see? Not you and I, but only We."

angel OF LIGHT

It's hard to see angels, although I've stared at their pictures for hours. Some people can see them without pictures, and they tell interesting tales. Guardian angels are all female, for instance, which didn't surprise me once I found out. A birth angel, recruited from the younger ranks, attends every baby when it appears, while another angel, older but not grim, helps the dying to leave this world without grief or pain.

You can pray to the angels and they will listen, but the best way to call them, I am told, is to laugh. Angels respond to delight, because that is what they're made of. In fact, when people's minds are clouded by anger or hatred, no angel can reach them.

Not all angels have wings—so the visionaries claim—but those who do can unfurl a span of golden feathers stretching over the entire world. If you had eyes that could look straight into the sun, you would see an overwhelming angel presiding there; a more serene one smiles out from the face of the moon.

Angels spend their entire lives, which are forever, spinning around the Creator's throne, singing His praise. People with keen ears have listened in. The harmonies of the angelic choir are incredibly complex, they say, but the rhythm is simple. "It's mostly march time," one eavesdropper affirmed. For some reason, that fact is almost the best I have learned so far.

After a while it got lonely hearing about angels you couldn't see for yourself. When an angel-watcher heard that, she was shocked. "Not see?" she said. "But you have an angel in you. Everybody does. I can see it right now, and I thought you could, too." "No," I said sadly, and I asked what it looked like. "Did it look like me?"

"Well, yes and no," the angel-watcher mysteriously answered. "It all depends on what you think you are. Your angel is a speck of light perched at the very center of your heart. It is smaller than an atom, but just wait. Once you get close to it, your angel will expand. The closer you come, the more it will grow, until finally, in a burst of light, you will see your angel in its true shape, and at that very instant, you will also see yourself."

So now I am looking for my angel all the time. I sit silently, turning my gaze inward. It wasn't long before I caught a glimpse of something. "Is that you, Angel, holding a candle?" One flicker and it was gone. Yet that was enough to set my heart wildly beating. Next time my angel will be waving a lamp, then holding a torch aloft, then lighting a bonfire.

That's what the angel-watcher promised, and now that I have caught sight of glory, I know enough to believe.

I *searched* FOR MY STAR

When I was little I used to lie on my back in the grass at night. I began to tell one star from another and wished that one of them could be mine, like an imaginary friend.

First I picked the Pole Star, because it is the easiest for a child to find, once you know that the Big Dipper is about to catch it. But I wanted my star to be a moving star, and not such a constant one. Besides, the sailors at sea would be lost without the Pole Star to guide them.

Next I picked out two special stars in the heart of the Swan. All the other stars looked white—but these were bright blue and gold. They reminded me of twin jewels, but before I could choose, I stopped. They belonged to each other, and it wouldn't be fair to take just one.

Orion's belt caught my eye for a moment, but I'm not a hunter. I had better leave the Dog Star alone, too, with its nose pressed to the celestial trail and its tail thumping the sky.

Last of all I turned to my favorites, the Seven Sisters. To me they were like elegant ladies getting ready for a ball, wrapped in a gossamer blue cloud. But who has the heart to tear seven sisters apart?

My game taught me a lot about the night sky, but I was growing up. The whole idea of having my own star faded, and it was hard to remember if I had ever chosen one in the end. People began to tell me that the word "star" meant something quite different. I half believed them, then one night I was tossing in bed, hurt and worried. My heart felt heavy with troubles. Stumbling to my feet, I looked out the window. Thick clouds masked the midnight sky. No stars!

I trembled to think of a world without stars. No guide for the sailor to trust at sea, no jewels to dazzle our sense of beauty, no hunter pointing to the next horizon, no lovely ladies trailing perfume to heaven's ballroom. But all around the globe, the air is so dirty and the lights from cities are so bright that for some people few stars can be seen anymore. A generation of children may grow up seeing a blank sky and asking, "Did there used to be stars there?"

Let's give them back the sky and let's do it now—before it's too late. I'm going to search for my star until I find it. It's hidden in the drawer of innocence, wrapped in a scarf of wonder. I'll need a map to tell me which hole it should fill, and that will be a small one. But there are nearly five billion of us on earth, and we all need the sky. Find your star and throw it up to heaven. You still have it, don't you?

A *child* IS A SONG

When children listen to music, they don't just listen. They melt into the melody and flow with the rhythm. Something inside starts to unfold its wings—soon the child and the music are one. I feel that way, too, in the presence of music, and my best moments of creativity have often been spent with children. When I am around them, music comes to me as easily as breathing.

Each song is a child I nourish and give my love to. But even if you have never written a song, your life is a song. How can it not be? In wave after wave, Nature caresses you—the rhythm of each dawn and each sunset is part of you, the falling rain touches your soul, and you see yourself in the clouds that are playing tag with the sun. To live is to be musical, starting with the blood dancing in your veins. Everything living has a rhythm. To feel each one, softly and attentively, brings out its music.

Do you feel your music?

Children do, but once we grow up, life becomes a burden and a chore, and the music grows fainter. Sometimes the heart is so heavy that we turn away from it and forget that its throbbing is the wisest message of life, a wordless message that says, "Live, be, move, rejoice—you are alive!" Without the heart's wise rhythm, we could not exist.

When I begin to feel a little tired or burdened, children revive me. I turn to them for new life, for new music. Two brown eyes look at me so deeply, so innocently, and inside I murmur, "This child is a song." It is so true and direct an experience that instantly I realize again, "I am a song also." I am back to myself once more.

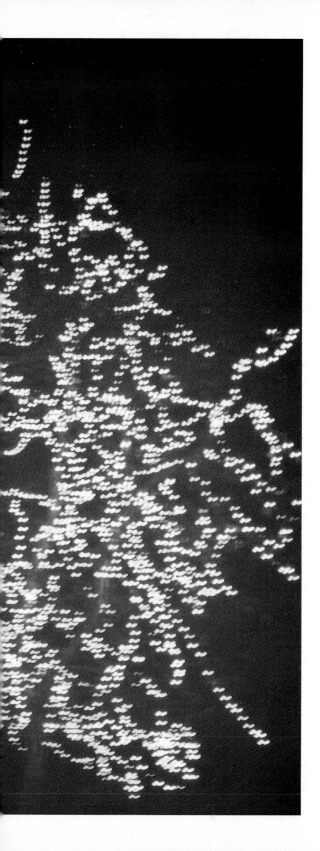

CHILD OF *innocence*

Child of innocence, I miss your sunny days
We joyously frolicked in extended plays
Ever since you've left the scene
The streets are lonely, dark, and mean

Child of innocence, return to me now
With your simple smile show them how
This world once again can respond to your glance
And heartbeats flutter to the rhythm of your dance

Child of innocence, your elegance, your beauty
Beckons me now beyond the call of duty
Come fly with me far and above
Over the mountains in the land of love

Child of innocence, messenger of joy
You've touched my heart without a ploy
My soul is ablaze with a flagrant fire
To change this world is my deepest desire.

WILL *you* BE THERE?

Hold me like the river Jordan
And I will then say to thee
You are my friend
Carry me like you are my brother
Love me like a mother
Will you be there?

When weary tell me will you hold me?
When wrong will you mold me?
When lost will you find me?
But they told me a man should be faithful
And walk when not able
And fight till the end
But I'm only human

Everyone's trying to control me
Seems that the world's got a role for me
I'm so confused
Will you show to me
You'll be there for me
And care enough to bear me?

Hold me, show me
Lay your head lowly
Gently and boldly
Carry me there
I'm only human

Hold me, show me
Lay your head lowly
Gentle and boldly
Carry me there
I'm only human

Carry, carry
Carry me boldly
Gently and slowly
Carry me there
I'm only human

Knead me
Love me and feed me
Kiss me and free me
And I will feel blessed

Lonely
When I'm cold and lonely
And needing you only
Will you still care?
Will you be there?

Save me
Heal me and bathe me
Softly you say to me
I will be there
But will you be there?

Hold me
Hug me and shield me
Touch me and heal me
I know you care
But will you be there?

Lonely
When I'm cold and lonely
(I get lonely sometimes, I get lonely)
And needing you only

Will you still care?
Will you be there?

Carry
Carry me boldly
Gently and slowly
Carry me there

Knead me
Love me and feed me
Kiss me and free me
And I will be blessed

Call me
Save me and face me

Bless me and say to me
I will be there
I know you care

Save me
Heal me and bathe me
Softly you say to me
I will be there
But will you be there?

Feed me
Feed me and soothe me
When I'm lonely and hungry
Will you still share?
Will you still care?

Nurse me
Soothe me, don't leave me
When I'm hurting and bleeding

Bruised and bare
Will you still care?

Kiss me
Face me and kiss me
And when my heart is breaking
Will you still care?
Will you be here?

Lift me
Lift me up carefully
I'm weary and falling
I know you're there
But do you still care?

part 2

magical CHILD

Magical child once felt a twinge
A faint recollection, a memory unhinged
In the colors, the forms, the hue
There seemed a mystery with a subtle clue
Behind the wind, the storm, the gale
Within the shroud, beyond the veil
Hidden from view in a wondrous pattern
There seemed a force that he could not fathom
Its music and cadence were playful and sweet
He danced in bliss to its throbbing beat
He did not mind either cold or heat
On the mountain high was his royal seat

Strangers came and scorned his joy
With ridicule and banter they tried to destroy
What in their minds was a skillful play
With cruel darts they tried to plunder
To suffocate and strangle his innocent wonder
Fighting hard, despite their blunder
Again and again to steal his thunder
Despite their attacks, they could not break

With all their barbs, they could not take
God's gift of love, which they could not fake
Not knowing his strength or what he sought to seek
They complained aloud and called him a freak

But the mysterious force just kept its hold
Magical child grew brave and bold
Diving deep into his soul
In exquisite ecstasy he discovered his role
In his Self was infinite scope
This mysterious force was mankind's hope
Piercing through that mask of Being
In that silence beyond all seeing
Was a field with a different story
A field of power, of awesome glory
With other children, if unfurled
Its tidal wave would change the world

Magical child was ready to bow
Sow the seed, pick up the plough
With effortless ease, without a sigh
Without a tear, without a cry
With silent perfection
Under God's direction
To sing together as one race
Stem the tide, transform this place

Magical children, don't worry how
Don't delay, this moment's now.

ARE YOU *listening?*

Who am I?
Who are you?
Where did we come from?
Where are we going?
What's it all about?
Do you have the answers?

Immortality's my game
From Bliss I came
In Bliss I am sustained
To Bliss I return
If you don't know it now
It's a shame
Are you listening?

This body of mine
Is a flux of energy
In the river of time
Eons pass, ages come and go
I appear and disappear
Playing hide-and-seek
In the twinkling of an eye

I am the particle
I am the wave
Whirling at lightning speed
I am the fluctuation
That takes the lead
I am the Prince
I am the Knave
I am the doing
That is the deed
I am the galaxy, the void of space
In the Milky Way
I am the craze

I am the thinker, the thinking, the thought
I am the seeker, the seeking, the sought
I am the dewdrop, the sunshine, the storm
I am the phenomenon, the field, the form
I am the desert, the ocean, the sky
I am the Primeval Self
In you and I

Pure unbounded consciousness
Truth, existence, Bliss am I
In infinite expressions I come and go
Playing hide-and-seek
In the twinkling of an eye
But immortality's my game

Eons pass
Deep inside
I remain
Ever the same
From Bliss I came
In Bliss I am sustained

Join me in my dance
Please join me now
If you forget yourself
You'll never know how
This game is played
In the ocean bed of Eternity

Stop this agony of wishing
Play it out
Don't think, don't hesitate
Curving back within yourself
Just create . . . just create

Immortality's my game
From Bliss I came
In Bliss I'm sustained
To Bliss I return
If you don't know it now
It's a shame
Are you listening?

BREAKING *free*

All this hysteria, all this commotion
Time, space, energy are just a notion
What we have conceptualized we have created
All those loved, all those hated

Where is the beginning, where's the end
Time's arrow, so difficult to bend
Those broken promises, what they meant
Those love letters, never sent

ONCE *we* WERE THERE

Before the beginning, before the violence
Before the anguish of the broken silence
A thousand longings, never uttered
Pangs of sorrow, brutally smothered

But I have chosen to break and be free
Cut those ties, so I can see
Those bonds that imprisoned me in memories of pain
Those judgments, interpretations that cluttered my brain

Those festering wounds that lingered have gone
In their place a new life has dawned
That lonely child, still clutching his toy
Has made his peace, discovered his joy

Where time is not, immortality's clear
Where love abounds, there is no fear
The child has grown to weave his magic
Left behind
His life of sorrow, once so tragic

He is now, ready to share
Ready to love, ready to care
Unfold his heart, with nothing to spare
Join him now, if you dare

heaven IS HERE

You and I were never separate
It's just an illusion
Wrought by the magical lens of
Perception

There is only one Wholeness
Only one Mind
We are like ripples
In the vast Ocean of Consciousness

Come, let us dance
The Dance of Creation
Let us celebrate
The Joy of Life

The birds, the bees
The infinite galaxies
Rivers, Mountains
Clouds and Valleys
Are all a pulsating pattern
Living, breathing
Alive with cosmic energy

Full of Life, of Joy
This Universe of Mine
Don't be afraid

To know who you are
You are much more
Than you ever imagined

You are the Sun
You are the Moon
You are the wildflower in bloom
You are the Life-throb
That pulsates, dances
From a speck of dust
To the most distant star

And you and I
Were never separate
It's just an illusion
Wrought by the magical lens of
Perception

Let us celebrate
The Joy of Life
Let us dance
The Dance of Creation

Curving back within ourselves
We create
Again and again
Endless cycles come and go
We rejoice
In the infinitude of Time

There never was a time
When I was not
Or you were not
There never will be a time
When we will cease to be

Infinite   Unbounded
In the Ocean of Consciousness
We are like ripples
In the Sea of Bliss

You and I were never separate
It's just an illusion
Wrought by the magical lens of
Perception

Heaven is Here
Right now is the moment
of Eternity
Don't fool yourself
Reclaim your Bliss

Once you were lost
But now you're home
In a nonlocal Universe
There is nowhere to go
From Here to Here
Is the Unbounded
Ocean of Consciousness
We are like ripples
In the Sea of Bliss

Come, let us dance
The Dance of Creation
Let us celebrate
The Joy of Life

And
You and I were never separate
It's just an illusion
Wrought by the magical lens of
Perception

Heaven is Here
Right now, this moment of Eternity
Don't fool yourself
Reclaim your Bliss

QUANTUM *leap*

I looked for you in hill and dale
I sought for you beyond the pale
I searched for you in every nook and cranny
My probing was at times uncanny
But everywhere I looked I found
I was just going round and round
In every storm, in every gale
I could hear your silent tale

You appeared wherever I went
In every taste, in every scent
I thought I was in a trance
In every quiver I felt your dance
In every sight I saw your glance
You were there, as if by chance

Even so, I have faltered
Despite the fact, my life has altered
All my doubts were struggles in vain
Of judgments made in memories of pain
Only now, by letting go
I can bask in your glow
No matter where I stray or flow
I see the splendor of your show
In every drama I am the actor
In every experience the timeless factor

In every dealing, every deed
You are there, as the seed
I know now, for I have seen
What could have happened could have been
There is no need to try so hard
For in your sleeve you hold the card
For every fortune, every fame
The Kingdom's here for us to claim
In every fire, every hearth
There's a spark gives new birth

To all those songs never sung
All those longings in hearts still young
Beyond all hearing, beyond all seeing
In the core of your Being
Is a field that spans infinity
Unbounded pure is the embryo of divinity
If we could for one moment BE
In an instant we would see
A world where no one has suffered or toiled
Of pristine beauty never soiled
Of sparkling waters, singing skies
Of hills and valleys where no one dies

That enchanted garden, that wondrous place
Where we once frolicked in times of grace
In ourselves a little deep
In that junkyard in that heap
Beneath that mound of guilt and sorrow
Is the splendor of another tomorrow
If you still have promises to keep
Just take that plunge, take that leap.

THAT *One* IN THE MIRROR

I wanted to change the world, so I got up one morning and looked in the mirror. That one looking back said, "There is not much time left. The earth is wracked with pain. Children are starving. Nations remain divided by mistrust and hatred. Everywhere the air and water have been fouled almost beyond help. Do something!"

That one in the mirror felt very angry and desperate. Everything looked like a mess, a tragedy, a disaster. I decided he must be right. Didn't I feel terrible about these things, too, just like him? The planet was being used up and thrown away. Imagining earthly life just one generation from now made me feel panicky.

It was not hard to find the good people who wanted to solve the earth's problems. As I listened to their solutions, I thought, "There is so much good will here, so much concern." At night before going to bed, that one in the mirror looked back at me seriously. "Now we'll get somewhere," he declared. "If everybody does their part."

But everybody didn't do their part. Some did, but were they stopping the tide? Were pain, starvation, hatred, and pollution about to be solved? Wishing wouldn't make it so—I knew that. When I woke up the next morning, that one in the mirror looked confused. "Maybe it's hopeless," he whispered. Then a sly look came into his eyes, and he shrugged. "But you and I will survive. At least we are doing all right."

I felt strange when he said that. There was something very wrong here. A faint suspicion came to me, one that had never dawned so clearly before. What if that one in the mirror isn't me? He feels separate. He sees problems "out there" to be solved. Maybe they will be, maybe they won't. He'll get along. But I don't feel that way—those problems aren't "out there," not really. I feel them inside me. A child crying in Ethiopia, a sea gull struggling pathetically in an oil spill, a mountain gorilla being mercilessly hunted, a teenage soldier trembling with terror when he hears the planes fly over: Aren't these happening in me when I see and hear about them?

The next time I looked in the mirror, that one looking back had started to fade. It was only an image after all. It showed me a solitary person enclosed in a neat package of skin and bones. "Did I once think you were me?" I began to wonder. I am not so separate and afraid. The pain of life touches me, but the joy of life is so much stronger. And it alone will heal. Life is the healer of life, and the most I can do for the earth is to be its loving child.

That one in the mirror winced and squirmed. He hadn't thought so much about love. Seeing "problems" was much easier, because love means complete self-honesty. Ouch!

"Oh, friend," I whispered to him, "do you think anything can solve problems without love?" That one in the mirror wasn't sure. Being alone for so long, not trusting others and being trusted by others, it tended to detach itself from the reality of life. "Is love more real than pain?" he asked.

"I can't promise that it is. But it might be. Let's discover," I said. I touched the mirror with a grin. "Let's not be alone again. Will you be my partner? I hear a dance starting up. Come." That one in the mirror smiled shyly. He was realizing that we could be best friends. We could be more peaceful, more loving, more honest with each other every day.

Would that change the world? I think it will, because Mother Earth wants us to be happy and to love her as we tend her needs. She needs fearless people on her side, whose courage comes from being part of her, like a baby who is brave enough to walk because Mother is holding out her arms to catch him. When that one in the mirror is full of love for me and for him, there is no room for fear. When we were afraid and panicky, we stopped loving this life of ours and this earth. We disconnected. Yet how can anybody rush to help the earth if they feel disconnected? Perhaps the earth is telling us what she wants, and by not listening, we fall back on our own fear and panic.

One thing I know: I never feel alone when I am earth's child. I do not have to cling to my personal survival as long as I realize, day by day, that all of life is in me. The children and their pain; the children and their joy. The ocean swelling under the sun; the ocean weeping with black oil. The animals hunted in fear; the animals bursting with the sheer joy of being alive.

This sense of "the world in me" is how I always want to feel. That one in the mirror has his doubts sometimes. So I am tender with him. Every morning I touch the mirror and whisper, "Oh, friend, I hear a dance. Will you be my partner? Come."

LOOK AGAIN, *baby* SEAL

One of the most touching nature photographs is of a baby fur seal lying on the ice alone. I'm sure you have seen it—the picture seems to be all eyes, the trusting dark eyes of a small animal gazing up at the camera and into your heart. When I first looked at them, the eyes asked, "Are you going to hurt me?" I knew the answer was yes, because thousands of baby seals were being killed every year.

Many people were touched by one baby seal's helplessness. They gave money to save the seals, and public awareness started to shift. As I returned to the picture, those two wide eyes began to say something different. Now they asked, "Do you know me?" This time I didn't feel so much heartache as when I felt the violence man inflicts upon animals. But I realized that there was still a big gap. How much did I really know about life on earth? What responsibility did I feel for creatures outside my little space? How could I lead my life so that every cell of living matter was also benefited?

Everyone who began to wonder about these things found, I think, that their feelings were shifting away from fear toward more closeness with life as a whole. The beauty and wonder of life began to seem very personal; the possibility of making the planet a garden for all of us to grow in began to dawn. I looked into the eyes of the baby seal, and for the first time they smiled. "Thank you," they said. "You have given me hope."

Is that enough? Hope is such a beautiful word, but it often seems very fragile. Life is still being needlessly hurt and destroyed. The image of one baby seal alone on the ice or one baby girl orphaned in war is still frightening in its helplessness. I realized that nothing would finally save life on earth but trust in life itself, in its power to heal, in its ability to survive our mistakes and welcome us back when we learn to correct those mistakes.

With these thoughts in my heart, I looked at the picture again. The seal's eyes seemed much deeper now, and I saw something in them that I had missed before: unconquerable strength. "You have not hurt me," they said. "I am not one baby alone. I am life, and life can never be killed. It is the power that brought me forth from the emptiness of space; it cared for me and nourished my existence against all dangers. I am safe because I am that power. And so are you. Be with me, and let us feel the power of life together, as one creature here on earth."

Baby seal, forgive us. Look at us again and again to see how we are doing. Those men who raise their clubs over you are also fathers and brothers and sons. They have loved and cared for others. One day they will extend that love to you. Be sure of it and trust.

THE DREAM CONTINUES ...

photo credits:

Dilip Mehta
Sam Emerson
Jonathan Exley
Greg Gorman

paintings by:

David Nordahl
Nate Giorgio

Special thanks to Sam Emerson